10 Most Effective Ways to Reignite *Self-Love*

"You are good enough for right now"

By

Rasheem Mays-Fowler

COPY RIGHT DISCLAIMER

Although the publisher and the author have made every effort to ensure that the information in this book was correct at press time and while this publication is designed to provide accurate information in regard to the subject matter covered, the publisher and the author assume no responsibility for errors, inaccuracies, omissions, or any other inconsistencies herein and hereby disclaim any liability to any party for any loss, damage, or disruption caused by errors or omissions, whether such errors or omissions result from negligence, accident, or any other cause.

The publisher and the author advise you to take full responsibility for your safety and know your limits. Before practicing the skills described in this book, be sure that your equipment is well maintained and do not take risks beyond your level of experience, aptitude, training, and comfort level.

The publisher and the author make no guarantees concerning the level of success you may experience by following the advice and strategies contained in this book, and you accept the risk that results will differ for everyone

This publication is meant as a source of valuable information for the reader, however it is not meant as a substitute for direct expert assistance. If such a level of assistance is required, the services of a competent professional should be sought.

ISBN: 978-1-7379347-0-7 Paperback

ISBN: 978-1-7379347-1-4 E-Book

For rights and permissions, please contact:

Rasheem Mays Fowler

TheAuthor@SheemOne.com

Dedication

Thank you to Kerra and Kade for giving me space to create and radiate my creativity. You two are my nucleus. Thank you, Kathy, for oiling the engines of my mind to keep me travelling to knowledge. To my father, siblings, bomb squad Bethea hall brothers, clubhouse family and friends. Thank you for all the wisdom and conversations that elevated my mind to have the courage to author this book.

Contents

Introduction

We do not choose our beginning, but we can make positive adjustments along the journey. This book is a reminder of the power within. We all need to be constantly reminded and refueled with the tools that bring out the best of our contributions to the universe and humanity. Seeking balance always starts with one side too high and one side too low. How will you stand firm?

1

The Interview

I unlocked secrets of myself when I tapped back into the source from which I came. I grew up in a single-parent home. My father walked out on us. However, there are many scenarios. Your parents could have been on drugs, abusive, absent because of their youth, their work, or sickness. To unlock the best secrets of yourself, you should interview your parents.

Have you ever thought about interviewing your parents/guardians? This is a MUST to break generational curses. You are no longer in a child's place. Life experiences have given you more understanding of adult pressures and your knowledge of the history and trials people went through. Write a list of questions for your parents and engage them in a true adult conversation.

Will you allow your parents to be better grandparents?

Will you allow closure?
Will you face your anxiety?

I did this:

Liberation: the word I use for the feelings I have. The first question I asked was;

Why did you Leave?

What would be your first question?
How ready are you to hear the answers?

I highly recommend this process.
It is a challenging job. It is pressure.

Remember, your parents have a STORY too. They are not just Mommy and Daddy.

There are things they do not know; things they failed to communicate; things they gave up; goals they will never reach, and pain they left unattended.

2

What are the Voices?

Affirmations as soon as your eyes open.
WHAT ARE THE VOICES? WHAT ARE THEY SAYING? / YOU ARE THE CREATOR OF YOUR REALITY.

As soon as you open your eyes, declare to the universe who you are and who you are becoming.

Start with small claims to the universe.

Remember, the more specific the claims, the greater the manifestation.

You must speak to the present; Be Positive and Be Specific.

In efforts to discipline your intentions and actions. Use an item in your vision that reminds you of

dedication to this process.

You must gain control of your Quad energy.

The four components that exert will power and ultimate confidence.

- Physical Energy
- Mental Energy
- Emotional Energy
- Action Energy

> Physical Energy - Look around wherever you are now and understand that everything you see started as an idea; in the mind first; then develops into a tangible asset; a creation, and miracles.

You must buy into your own nature. You must settle into a pure conviction that your thoughts are miracles.

> Mental Energy -Activate your Dopamine for Pleasure and Motivation

Here are some samples to increase - Dopamine

Exercise Often

Get Enough Sleep

Listen to Music / Motivational Tapes

> Dopamine allows us to feel bliss, pleasure, euphoria, and motivation.

Emotional Energy - Activate your Oxytocin

Here are some samples to increase Oxytocin

Make your conversations count.
Cook (and eat) with someone you care about.
Have sex.
Cuddle or hug.
Do something nice for someone.

Oxytocin – the love hormone – creates intimacy, trust and builds strong and healthy relationships.

Have you been yearning for more intimacy and found yourself overcompensating, engaging in any of these categories to find balance? Upon my research on this subject, I realized I have. Reaccess this information and realize you have done things to activate these levels without knowing it. You are truly looking to raise your Oxytocin.

Your Body possesses all things needed to unlock your full control over what's created in your mind to manifest in the physical. '

Physical Action, Emotional Action, Mental Action, and Action Energy

What do you REALLY want?

Do YOU know? Write down what you need right now.

Do you not have a clue?

Start with these.

"I am good enough right now"
"My Best will always get Better"
"I have all the tools I need to beat this; I just have to think"

3

Get Off Autopilot

Talk to yourself. Dig for accountability. Accept all the terms of your personality. "GET OFF AUTOPILOT"

When was the last time you looked in the mirror? No, really looked in the mirror. Evaluate your character as you do with friends, co-workers, strangers, and family.

Do you just brush your teeth, wash your face, etc. without looking into your own eyes, your trauma, your drama, beauty, success, and learning moments? Can you have a real conversation with yourself, accepting all the layers of your personality?

Are you afraid?
Are you ashamed?
Who are you?

What do you see?
Are you available for Correction?

You must DO THE WORK!

The Key is accepting all of yourself. Accept what is on the surface to your deepest bone in the closet.

Start shedding your skin. Realize the moment you start healing.

These conversations with self-help you control your emotions. Interacting with people, good or bad, will not control your emotional reactions.

You are mastering your processing stage.

Do I need to be here?
Is this healthy for me?

You learn to own who you totally are.

You learn all your actions and steps starting with your Accountability.

They are only a few moments in accountability within your life, that you are not responsible.

OWN IT AND TAKE CONTROL.

Taking control means you start to know yourself. You hone in on your likes and dislikes. You find a consistent system to keep yourself in growth. You now can make demands of yourself and set accurate standards for all future relationships.

We all need to shed our skin and grow.

This comes with major work and the consistent peeling of layers.

Don`t be afraid of correction and seek professional help.

4

Who Plans for you?

Routine/Plan. Reduce your news, unless you work in the news

How predictable are you?
Do you plan down to the minutes of your day?
1440 minutes (about 1 day)
How many do you have unplanned?
How many minutes do people take from you that do not benefit your goals or growth?

My brother Karte`once gave me some vital entrepreneurial advice.

If you have a 9-5 and that is not your final destination, make sure you use that job to crowdfund the career you want for the Second and Third act of your life.

A job is simply renting you and in return, they pay you with a tool called money. This tool helps you balance your life, allows you to assign tasks to others, and gives you more free time. This is one of the many ways to complete more goals in a 24-hour period.

For Example: You pay someone to cut your grass or in any other arena to save you time for other things on your agenda.

> Time: You must plan to have it, or the world will plan for you.

Allocate time for self-love, family, and purpose building,

Are you happy with where your time goes?

This discipline focuses on routine, discipline over motivation, it is not about how you feel or what mood you are in. You must stay the course and not worry about other people's feelings about you.

Keep hustling.
Stick to the routine.
Associate yourself with the people in your Vision.

I acknowledge things that happen unexpectedly.

I recommend you put your mind in the space where most put their jobs.

Random inconvenient things happen in life consistently.

> One thing holds true; people often rush back to work. They find that mental space to keep working. Are you that for self-love? If life knocks you off your feet. Do not delay getting back to your routine. Success is on Purpose. Don`t work for it. Work toward it. Do not be afraid to eliminate things that steal time from you. Things that hinder your focus from being better.

HOW MUCH FREE TIME DOES THE AVERAGE PERSON HAVE?

5 hours per day.

The average person spends 3 hours, 13 minutes each day doing 1 unnecessary activity.

The plan for yourself should be detailed down the minute as if you were president of the United States. "You are worth it" "You are Good Enough for right now" "Your best will always get better"

There are many things that take time from you. Kids, other family members, A demanding job, spouse, toxic friends, group chats on social media. Are you scrolling; looking at other people's lives and not working on your own?

All these things do not prioritize your self-love unless you demand it.

You are better to serve others when whole.

Planning will always happen in life.

Will you control the terms and conditions?

Success can be on purpose.

5

How Many Days Lost?

We spoke about routine and planning. Within the planning comes the energy flow and execution.

Now that you have planned your day and started your affirmations, it is time to cut out the negative habits and people who do not feed your self-love standards.

The Five Love languages are a suitable place to start.

Taking the online quiz and reading about The Five Love Languages will send you into a higher vibration of self-love and self-demands. No need for expectations, only demands in communication.

When you start to understand what type of love fills you up, it is time to demand that from the friends, lovers, coworkers, and family around you.

DO NOT BE AFRAID TO CUT PEOPLE OUT OF YOUR LIFE.

Have accountability, they are only there because you allow it.

Do you feel the need for that toxic energy to function?
Are you really trying to save them?
Are you using them to fuel your thirst for toxins?

It is a two-way street.

Family and Friends who cannot feed what you demand should be awarded little to no time for your mental real estate.

Warning do not make mistakes or corrections with people not meeting your demands. The people who love you will notice your growth and accept it. Those people will also offer you corrections about your character shortcomings. Be open to hearing the message. Not the messenger or their character.

Take advice and fact check. Adjust and keep building.

Remember the love language you demand may not be the love language you give out to friends, family, or spouse/partner.

You must communicate and set the table for yourself and that person. What is their love language?

You should be willing to give the reciprocity you demand.

It is a two-way street

How much time do you give to so-called friends that do not lift a finger to help you grow to your higher self?
Are you that Friend?
Do they ignore your growth?
Do they honor your demanding work?
Do they consistently put you in situations that steal your time and focus?

Where are you trying to go?

No one can go with you, but good people can cheer you on while you run your self-love marathon.

If you give one hour a day for 365 days (about 12 months) to the wrong distraction, you have wasted 365 hours (about 2 weeks). That is 15 days (about 2 weeks) a year of your life you gave away.

Spend time with people and the atmosphere that keeps you illuminated and motivated.

Make Demands, Make Separations, Allow Correction, Modify and Grow.

6

Dormant Thoughts

Read books that attract you to change your subconscience.

Even after you make the necessary adjustment to cleanse your life of toxic distractions, you still can attract the same people back in your life repeatedly until you change your subconscious thoughts.

We all have reactions mostly molded over time from our experiences.

I encourage you to seek out the Subconscious Mind Test.

You can determine what you mostly feel or think when you are not actively thinking.

Does your natural reaction when angry, startled, or excited bring about a defensive surge?

A defense mechanism.

Do You feel on-edge around others for no apparent reason?
Do You often feel like an innocent victim?
Do You feel like the world is against you?
Do You tend to be critical and sarcastic?
Do You rarely accept blame (because you “haven't done anything wrong”)?

People underestimate the power of many phrases, but this is one of my favorites that I take seriously.

"I've Changed My Mind"

I have changed my mind. This statement is such a powerful development.

You start by expanding your imagination, experiences, and knowledge of other cultures.

Reading is more than fundamental

It is fun for the mental.

Invest in your mental real estate.

Start to read, that enhances you. Totally commit to new experiences. Give your mind a better imagination.

Listen to speeches and music while you sleep.

Invest in broadening the deepest parts of your thoughts.

You have the power to change your mind no matter what memories already exist. You can choose Kindness, listening with intent, responding in control and not in defense.

7

Own Your Discomfort

Find discomfort in your growth.

Do the things you do not want to do. Make a contract with yourself. Do not break it. Do not compromise. Why are you uncomfortable?

> WHAT ARE YOU NOT DOING? WHY DOES THAT MAKE YOU UNCOMFORTABLE?

Growing in self-love is nerve-racking. You are doing the things you do not want to do or feel.

How else would you explain taking this long to really commit to your evaluations? You are changing your Muscle Memory. It takes practice and consistency. You make excuses to stop before you reach your growth spurt.

The biggest secret that all great men know, is to do the things that make you uncomfortable. That is where real growth is.

Most of us have one or multiple things we talk ourselves out of every day that would be to our benefit, but we choose to procrastinate. We commit to our lazy stubborn feelings.

Whenever that feeling of discomfort or laziness strikes you, run toward the assignment.

That is where real growth is.

What makes you uncomfortable to try?
What makes you uncomfortable pushing past your physical limits?
Does your mind say STOP, or CONTINUE, you got this?
Does success scare you?

Build your courage. Start with the trivial things, or if you are an extremist like me, start with the hard ones.

Meet adversity with service and a smile.

Turn those nervous butterflies in your stomach into excitement.

Be overjoyed to show the universe what you know you are capable of and prepared to do.

OWN YOUR DISCOMFORT

8

Food is Medicine not for Celebrating

Do not celebrate with food.
Many of us celebrate with food.
Many of us eat and drink for other people's special occasions outside our discipline.

Forming one of the highest levels of self-love is food discipline.

Food is the real medicine. Listen to your body and research the healthy foods that give the nutrients to activate and boost your production volume.

Many of us randomize our food choices, leaving it up to our cravings to lead us.

What you eat and how much you eat should be routine and predictable.

Seek professional advice about meal prepping.

Read books about your blood type and body type.

See your physician and do an allergy test.

Know what is best for you. Do not rely on trial and error.

Be selfish about what you put in your body.

Confidence is the key ingredient in self-love. Your dopamine will shoot through the roof when you are taking the right steps to say NO; to the food at the celebration but still enjoy the event.

Can you stop celebrating with Food?
Can you break the constructs of food traditions?
Do you love yourself enough to go alone?

This with effective practice will give more access to finances.

Celebrate by spending the tool called money; assisting you to maintain consistent strategies to center yourself with the foods that give you the best vibes, energy, and overall health.

9

The Villain or The Mentor?

Find the person in your field or life goals and compete until you outwork them.

> FIND A VILLAIN; someone you are inspired by!

The Villain or The Mentor?
Who brings more out of you to compete?
Who teaches you about yourself more?

> FIND A MENTOR that inspires you or find a villain that keeps you fired up.

Competing is a way of life.

Looking for competition is a mental tool to sharpen attention to detail.

Study your rival, mentor, and self.

Do research on the people in your field. How do/did they maintain, develop, and fail? Keep what you need for your tool belt. Apply the work ethic needed to see predictable progress.

Once you have gotten all you need from that competitor, pick another of higher discipline.

Michael Jordan, arguably the greatest basketball player of his time played with a mental chip on his shoulder. He found ways to make his contemporaries the villain. He used it as fuel to stay FIRED UP!

When someone is your rival in a competition, you give it your all, desperately trying to outperform, Practice more and Study more than them. The recipe worked for MJ.

I challenge you to pick someone to compete against. They do not have to know your competing. They don`t even have to know you, but in your mind, you are competing and coming for their spot. Trust me, they know and respect that someone is competing. Someone is always coming for their spot and competing against them. Right now, someone is actively competing against you.

This self-love tactic helps you stay polished with high confidence and willpower.

At some point, talent and knowledge are equal.

The supreme power of self-love leverages the universe to perform miracles in your favor.

Have you chosen a Mentor?

Have you chosen a Villain?

Are you competing in all forms of Life?

The rewards are a side effect when you subscribe

to a healthy competitive pedigree.

10

The Infinite Honeymoon Phase

Think of when you are in the honeymoon stage of any relationship; when the energy is exactly right. It does not matter when you meet up, when you talk or how long you talk. You just want to be present in the melodic space of energy with that being.

Imagine that person was yourself. "You are good enough right now"

When was the last time you took yourself out on a date?
Did you get dressed up?
Did you go out to dinner?
Did you sit at a table and not at a Bar?
When you are alone on a date, the relevance of your spirit heightens to another level. You will do what your first thoughts process. No restrictions.

How could you ever tell someone how to treat you if you never treated yourself?

Your communication becomes direct. You can now educate, customize, and demand the energy around you.

Pay yourself

Relate to yourself

Date yourself

Do a staycation with yourself

There are tough questions that come next, but if you DO THE WORK, you absolutely will be operating on a higher form of universal energy

Would you date yourself?
Why don`t you date yourself?

If that depresses you or you find it dumb, are you saying you would not date you?

This is not a formal accusation nor is it validation for those who already date themselves.

This is a recap of steps One through Nine.
Being ourselves is priceless.
Just know "Your Best will always Get Better"

And "You are good enough for right now"

Take yourself out on a date once a week. Let your spirit guide you.

Freelance. Get dressed up. Go wherever YOU want. Liberate and refresh.

Enjoy YOU!

Conclusion

10 Most Effective Ways to Reignite Self Love

Take your time; Build up slowly; you have many levels of doubt to overcome, muscle memory to make new and renew.

The school structure was always a concept that most adults live today and do not notice. Most protest the relevant use of knowledge that is taught in school for later use in life, but I focus on the process. The time allocated we had to learn new skills.

Usually, you get to focus on each subject/skill for 45 mins to an hour. That is when extreme focus was sharpened and applied. Math time was Math, Gym time was Gym time. etc.

Applying the High School structure of class periods to rebuild and reshape your life is one of the ways I have been on my journey.

For Example: Below is how I allocate my time to apply constant growth in making success on purpose.

Homeroom: First thing in the morning before I start my work. I speak my affirmations with power and center myself.

Math: Focus of financial time for family finance, investments, and investment planning.

Science: Reading and Learning about the foods I eat and how do they affect my body as I get older.

Language Arts: I value the opportunity to see what new book will grow my imagination; what unfamiliar words I can add to my vocabulary, what new culture, new country, new location did I learn about, and what new manual gave me the knowledge to understand the full functions of a product.

Gym: My time to release the right chemicals in my body through exercise, facing the day with less stress and good vibes while maintaining the quality of my overall health.

Recess: I relax, get excited, and do research about where I am taking myself on a date this week.

Be the best in your class. Stick to your principles.
Put yourself in detention for correction.
Practice the right study habits for self.
You have the time for YOU. Will you allocate it?
REIGNITE YOUR SELF-LOVE.
Have the COURAGE to Love you.

PEACE AND BLESSINGS

CPSIA information can be obtained
at www.ICGtesting.com
Printed in the USA
BVHW042241120322
631351BV00016B/1433